What they don't tell you about

LIVING THINGS

By Bob Fowke

Dedicated to mousehogs - they don't exist,
but it would be good if they did.

*Hodder
Children's
Books*

a division of Hodder Headline plc

Hallo, my name's Dr Dandelion. I'm a biologist. That means I study living things; there's a lot of amazing creatures out there - and inside you. Come with me and we'll find out what life is really all about.

Produced by Fowke & Co. for Hodder Children's Books

Cover photo: False-colour scanning electron micrograph of the protozoan *Giardia lamblia*. Reproduced by courtesy of Chris Bjornberg/Science Photo Library.

Published by Hodder Children's Books 1997

0340 693495

Hodder Children's Books
a Division of Hodder Headline plc
338 Euston Road
London NW1 3BH

Printed and bound by Cox & Wyman Ltd, Reading, Berks
A Catalogue record for this book is available from the British Library

CONTENTS

WHAT A LIFE!
WHAT WE ARE - AND WHERE WE CAME FROM

I STINK THEREFORE I AM
NERVES AND SENSES

YOU ARE WHAT YOU EAT
FOOD - AND HOW WE GET THE MOST OUT OF IT

AN ATHLETE'S ARMPIT
YOUR SKIN - AND THE THINGS WHICH LIVE IN IT

STAND UP AND BE COUNTED
BAG OF SKIN SEEKS BONES AND MUSCLES
TO STAND UP IN

TAKE A DEEP BREATH!
WHY YOU BREATHE AND WHAT BLOOD DOES

OFF SICK
ILLNESSES AND HOW WE FIGHT THEM OFF

BABY BOOM!
HAVING BABIES - AND LOOKING AFTER THEM

Watch out for the *Sign of the Foot*! Whenever you see this sign in the book it means there are some more details at the *FOOT* of the page. Like here.

WHAT A LIFE!

WHAT WE ARE - AND WHERE WE CAME FROM

Let's start at the beginning.

PLANET EARTH A VERY LONG TIME AGO ...

A very small creature sloshes to and fro in warm, salty water near the shore of a vast ocean. It's all alone. There are no nasty sharks or big bad fish about to eat it.

This creature is just a blob of chemicals, the smallest possible speck of life. It has no mother or father, no brothers or sisters. It has been made by lifeless chemicals in the sea and the effect of sun or lightning.

It's so small you could never see it with your naked eye - but this one tiny blob is the ancestor of *all living things on planet Earth*.

Yes, most scientists think that we are all descended from a single blob of chemicals, which may have formed in the sea between 4,500 and 3,000 million years ago when the Earth was young. Such a very important blob needs a name - let's call it 'Fiona the First'.

STOP!

DR DISAGREE SAYS ...

The idea that life started in the sea is only a *hypothesis* , even if it's the most popular one among scientists. In science, hypotheses are tested by experiments, in order to prove them right or wrong. There's no direct proof of Fiona (4,000 million years is a very long time ago and Fiona would have been very small indeed), and scientists are still trying to create life in laboratory experiments. In fact some scientists say that life-chemicals may have come from outer space, or that life started in the warm water around underwater volcanoes.

Hypothesis (plural: *hypotheses*) comes from an old Greek word. It means a 'starting idea'.

ARE YOU ALIVE? A QUICK TEST

Fiona the First may have been tiny, but she, or rather *it*, was about to take over the world - because Fiona was able to grow and to make copies of itself. Fiona was *alive*. Making more individuals or *reproducing* is typical of living things. There are several other activities which all living things do, as well as reproducing themselves. Check which of these you do.

b Breathe c Pour d Grow

a Boil

e Take in food and water

f Move (even plants can move parts of themselves)

g Get rid of your waste products

h Reproduce (meaning to have children, if you're human)

i Make ripples when blown on

j Die

k Feel, or be sensitive to, things outside you

Answers   j - you were alive - now you're not!
b,d,e,f,g,h,k - if you do all these you must be alive.
a,c,i - you're probably a glass of water.

7

Fiona gets busy

It seems that Fiona was able to split in half, thus making two new Fionas which could split in half again and so on. A million years after the first oceans filled up with water, they were probably bubbling with Fiona-like creatures.

The Fionas ate each other and other chemicals as food. It seems that in some way, the chemicals in the Fionas were changed by the chemicals which they ate, as if some of the food chemicals became a permanent part of the Fiona. In this way new types of Fiona kept appearing as one generation gave way to the next.

The Fionas which filled the oceans were *cells*, the smallest unit of life in the world today. They would have been made up of a living skin or *cell membrane* with living stuff inside.

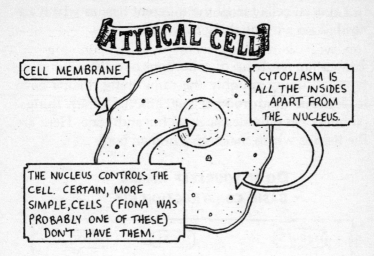

A TYPICAL CELL

CELL MEMBRANE

CYTOPLASM IS ALL THE INSIDES APART FROM THE NUCLEUS.

THE NUCLEUS CONTROLS THE CELL. CERTAIN, MORE SIMPLE, CELLS (FIONA WAS PROBABLY ONE OF THESE) DON'T HAVE THEM.

Gradually some of these cells joined up with each other forming two-celled then many-celled creatures. Now, up to 4,500 million years later, there are still some creatures which have only one cell, and some which have thousands, and some, like us, which have billions of cells.

HALLO HUMANS

There are in fact about ten trillion cells in the human body. Each one is mainly made up of salty water - the same sort of warm, salty water that Fiona lived in all those millions of years ago.

The truth is that each of us, like all living creatures, is basically just a huge pile of Fionas!

Or perhaps the parent cell and its 'child' never separated after reproducing - imagine being stuck to your mother for ever!

Unlike Fiona we have many different kinds of cell. We have special muscle cells and special blood cells, in fact special cells for all the different tissues which are needed for a living thing to work.

Tissues are made up of collections of cells of the same type, all doing roughly the same thing. Plants have leaf tissue and root tissue among other things. Animals have tissues such as fur and bone. Here are the tissues which make up a human body ...

DO IT YOURSELF HUMAN
– BASIC CONSTRUCTION KIT

Groups of tissues working together make up the *organs* (eg stomach and brain) which make the *systems* which keep living things alive. Animals have several systems. Here are two examples ...

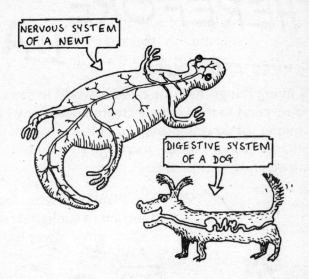

NERVOUS SYSTEM OF A NEWT

DIGESTIVE SYSTEM OF A DOG

I STINK THEREFORE I AM

NERVES AND SENSES

All living things 'feel' the outside world in some way and respond to it. In simple creatures this may be just a matter of keeping their mouth-parts open and noticing when some food gets in (and then remembering to close them!).

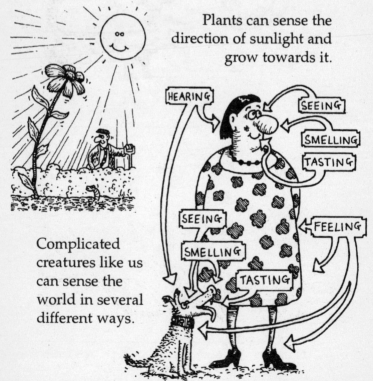

Plants can sense the direction of sunlight and grow towards it.

Complicated creatures like us can sense the world in several different ways.

HEARING

SEEING

SMELLING

TASTING

SEEING

SMELLING

TASTING

FEELING

You're So Brainy!

Your brain controls your body and nearly everything you do, but it's just a soft, squidgy mass of cells shut away in the dark cave of your head. It has no eyes or ears of its own, nor any way of telling what's going on outside. It has to rely on *nerve-messages* from other parts of your body to find out what's going on outside.

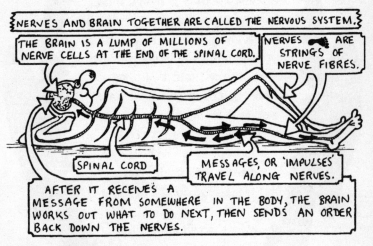

NERVES AND BRAIN TOGETHER ARE CALLED THE NERVOUS SYSTEM.

THE BRAIN IS A LUMP OF MILLIONS OF NERVE CELLS AT THE END OF THE SPINAL CORD.

NERVES ARE STRINGS OF NERVE FIBRES.

SPINAL CORD

MESSAGES, OR 'IMPULSES' TRAVEL ALONG NERVES.

AFTER IT RECEIVES A MESSAGE FROM SOMEWHERE IN THE BODY, THE BRAIN WORKS OUT WHAT TO DO NEXT, THEN SENDS AN ORDER BACK DOWN THE NERVES.

The largest nerve fibres of any living thing belong to the giant squid. Their nerves can be two centimetres across: human nerves are a thousand times smaller.

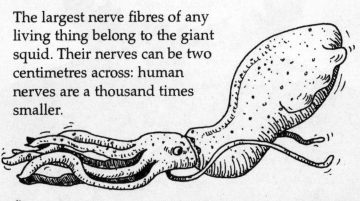

Erasistratus, an ancient Greek, thought that nerves were hollow tubes which carried messages in the form of 'nervous spirit' to the brain.

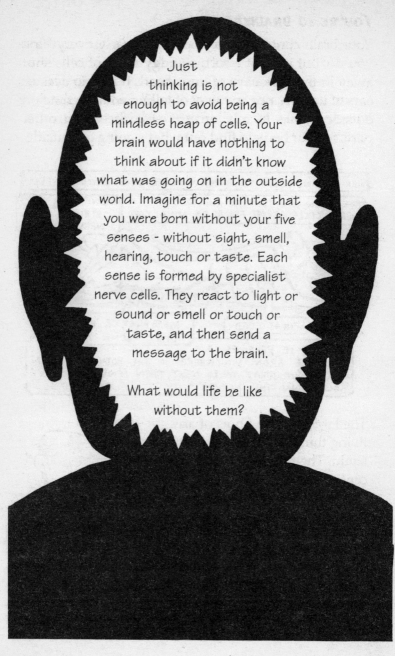

Just thinking is not enough to avoid being a mindless heap of cells. Your brain would have nothing to think about if it didn't know what was going on in the outside world. Imagine for a minute that you were born without your five senses - without sight, smell, hearing, touch or taste. Each sense is formed by specialist nerve cells. They react to light or sound or smell or touch or taste, and then send a message to the brain.

What would life be like without them?

SENSE NO. 1 - SMELL

Deep in the slimiest darkest depths of your nose there is a layer of special smell-cells which can detect chemicals in the air. The amount of smell-chemical can be tiny. For instance you can smell one little speck of vanilla-ice-cream-smell in 100,000,000,000 times as much air.

But that's nothing. People have a poor sense of smell compared to most other animals. We only have around five million smell-cells.

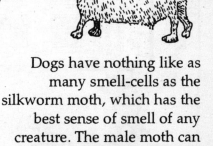

Dogs have about two hundred million smell-cells, which is why they smell things so much better than we do.

Dogs have nothing like as many smell-cells as the silkworm moth, which has the best sense of smell of any creature. The male moth can smell the female when she's eleven kilometres away.

Grass snakes 'smell' with their tongues. The flickering tongue picks out smell chemicals in the air and passes them to the mouth which 'tastes' them.

SMELL TEST

It's not just moths which can smell out males and females. Ninety-five per cent of humans can tell if someone is male or female just by smelling their breath (provided they haven't eaten anything smelly like strong cheese).

This head teacher is blind. But she's found a way to sort the boys from the girls!

We give off smell-chemicals all the time, in case you hadn't noticed. Here are a few of the more common human smell-chemicals:

Not everyone likes these smells which is why many people wear what the Germans used to call stinkon and the Romans called par fumar - or perfume as we call it today. In the Middle Ages most perfume smelled of oranges and was used to cover the smell of dirty bodies. Today there's a wider choice of perfumes.

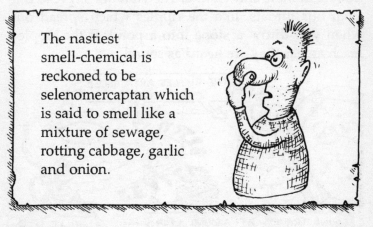

The nastiest smell-chemical is reckoned to be selenomercaptan which is said to smell like a mixture of sewage, rotting cabbage, garlic and onion.

Par fumar means 'by smoke' in Latin.

SENSE NO. 2 - HEARING

One of the really useful things about hearing is that people can hear things they can't see. You *can* give off a smell if you're lost in a wood and your parents can't see you, but it might be better to shout.

Our smell-cells detect real smell-chemicals in the air but our ears don't hear sound-chemicals. They hear air, because that's all sound is in most cases - air, moving.

When we speak or shout, we make the air in our throats tremble and vibrate. The vibrations spread out from our throats, like the ripples which spread out when you throw a stone into a pond. If the ripples reach an ear they are heard as sound.

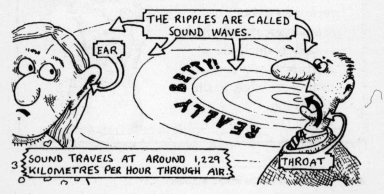

There are three parts to the human ear.

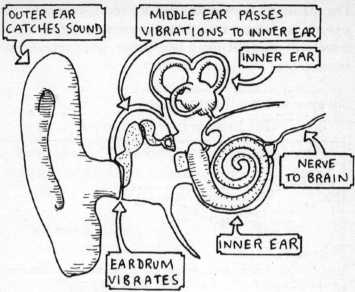

OUTER EAR CATCHES SOUND

MIDDLE EAR PASSES VIBRATIONS TO INNER EAR

INNER EAR

NERVE TO BRAIN

INNER EAR

EARDRUM VIBRATES

Sound travels through other materials as well as air. Whale songs can be heard by other whales hundreds of kilometres away through water.

EAR EAR

Snakes 'hear' through their jaw-bones. If a snake's head is off the ground, it will not be able to detect sounds.

Spiders and crickets have their ear-drums on their legs.

SENSE NO. 3 - SIGHT

The reason your parents can't see you if you're lost in a wood is because their eyes can only see light, which travels in straight lines and never goes round tree trunks.

But eyes do have their uses ...

THE JOURNEY OF A BIT OF LIGHT

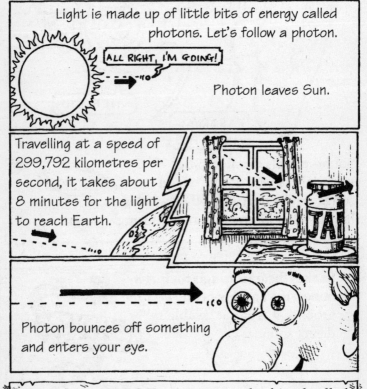

Light is made up of little bits of energy called photons. Let's follow a photon.

ALL RIGHT, I'M GOING!

Photon leaves Sun.

Travelling at a speed of 299,792 kilometres per second, it takes about 8 minutes for the light to reach Earth.

Photon bounces off something and enters your eye.

As early as 300 BC Erasistratus and a friend called Herophilus cut up the eyeballs of executed criminals. They thought that eyes send out beams of light in order to see things.

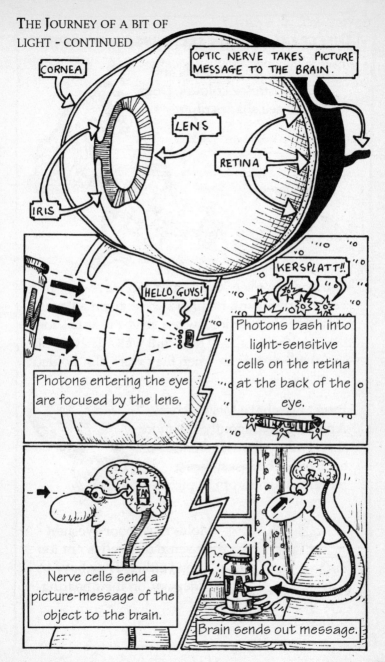

DIFFERENT ANIMALS SEE THINGS DIFFERENTLY

People, frogs, lizards and birds can see colours. Dogs only see shades of grey

Humans can't see X-rays, but monkeys can. In a recent experiment, monkeys were given a banana each time they noticed when an X-ray was shone through their cage. They did well. They could 'see' the X-rays even when they were blindfolded.

Insect eyes have lots of lenses. An average dragonfly has more than twenty thousand lenses on each eye. The insect sees a pattern of overlapping pictures.

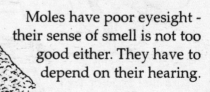

Moles have poor eyesight - their sense of smell is not too good either. They have to depend on their hearing.

A SENSIBLE DECISION

Sight, smell and hearing are our long-distance senses.

There are still two close-up senses - touch and taste.
And life wouldn't be much fun without them ...

SENSE NO. 4 - TOUCH

You've only got one pair of eyes, one pair of ears, one nose and one mouth.

Touch is different from the other senses, because you have an army of touch nerve endings *all over* your body - and even inside it. They're ready for action night and day. Whenever you touch something they send a message to your brain. But each touch nerve ending will react to just one type of feeling, either heat, cold, light touch, pressure or pain. So there's no point in putting a red-hot needle to a nerve that specialises in cold - it won't take any notice.

Imagine: you pick up a red hot poker and there's no sense of pain. The first you would know that something was wrong would be when a smell of burning flesh reached your nose. By the time you'd worked out that the smell wasn't coming from the cooker, you'd have fingers like roast sausages.

We need pain to warn us if something is wrong with our bodies - inside or out - even if we don't like it.

SENSE NO.5 - TASTE

When we chew or suck food, chemicals in the food ooze into our spit, also called saliva, and this spitty-food-mixture gets smeared over special taste-cells in the 'taste buds' on our tongues.

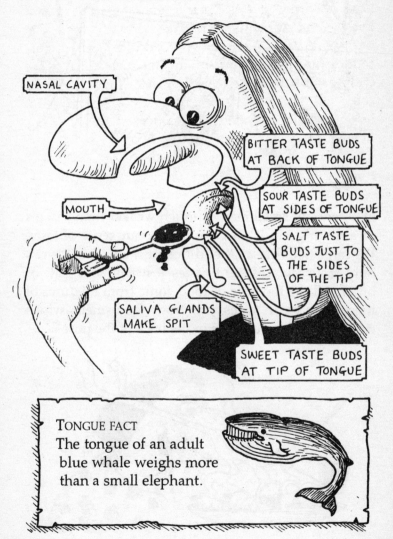

NASAL CAVITY

BITTER TASTE BUDS AT BACK OF TONGUE

SOUR TASTE BUDS AT SIDES OF TONGUE

MOUTH

SALT TASTE BUDS JUST TO THE SIDES OF THE TIP

SALIVA GLANDS MAKE SPIT

SWEET TASTE BUDS AT TIP OF TONGUE

TONGUE FACT
The tongue of an adult blue whale weighs more than a small elephant.

Our sense of smell may be much weaker than a dog's or a moth's, but it's a giant beside our sense of taste. We can smell *thousands* of different smells, but we can only taste *four* different tastes - sweet, sour, salt or bitter. All the flavours of food come from mixtures of these four basic tastes and from food-smells which drift up to the smell-cells in the back of the nose.

DR DANDELION'S DATA DETAILS

Check out this summary of nerves and senses.

All living things can sense the outside world in some way.

Humans have five senses - sight, smell, hearing, touch and taste.

Nerves and brain together are called the nervous system.

The human ear has three parts - inner, middle and outer.

Human taste buds can only taste four tastes.

YOU ARE WHAT YOU EAT

FOOD - AND HOW WE GET THE MOST OUT OF IT

All living things need food, or *nutrients*, in order to stay alive. How much food animals need depends on how big they are and how active.

Elephants eat up to half a tonne of food per day. This is nothing compared to the blue whale, which eats around four tonnes of tiny sea creatures per day.

Small creatures which rush around a lot have to eat vast quantities of food to gain enough energy. The Etruscan shrew eats three times its own weight in food per day, and it must have a meal every two hours or it dies.

Vampire bats take their food in liquid form - they need the blood of other animals, about a tablespoon per day!

Some animals, such as the koala bear, are very picky about what they eat.

The koala only likes the leaves of the eucalyptus tree, and will only eat the leaves of five out of 350 varieties of this tree.

Other animals, like us, can eat a wide range of foods.

Digestion

Running through your body is a group of squidgy organs , arranged like a long tube with your mouth at one end and your bottom at the other. This food-tube is called the *alimentary canal* . What it does is take food in at one end, squeeze out all the goodness and then get rid of the rubbish at the other end.

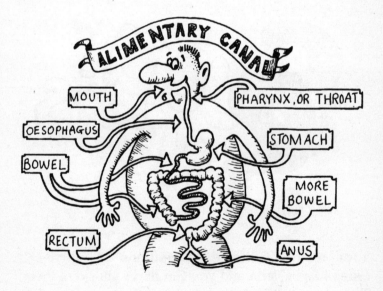

Organs are parts of the body such as the heart and the stomach which have special jobs to do to help keep the body alive.

Alimentum is Latin for food.

CHOMP CHOMP

The first step is to chew up the food and squidge it around with spit before swallowing it. Our normal chewing speed is about a hundred chomps per minute, and our teeth bite at a pressure of two hundred kilograms per square centimetre (and if that means nothing to you, try biting your tongue). The surface enamel on our teeth is the hardest thing in our bodies.

But although tooth enamel is very hard, nowadays it's not hard enough. There was a time when tooth rot was almost unknown; now you're lucky to reach old age with many teeth at all. The reason is simple:

Your teeth are home to millions of single-cell Fiona-like bacteria and you can never get rid of them. They love sugar better than anything and as they munch away they produce a strong waste acid, strong enough to dissolve the enamel which covers your teeth. And once the acid has eaten through the enamel, these vicious Fiona-like creatures cram into the gap and the next thing you know, the inside of your tooth is an oozy mess of micro-monsters.

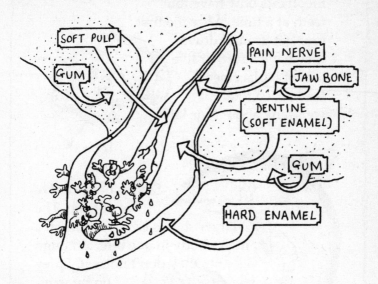

You can never get rid of them, but you can starve them:

Cut down on sweets.
Cut down on sweet drinks.
Brush your teeth.

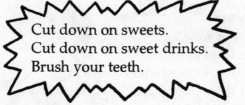

TOOTH FACT
Snails have 25,600 teeth. They can chew through almost anything they want to eat.

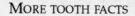

Elephants only have four teeth at a time. After the first four get ground down, they have a further five sets of replacement teeth, each tooth weighing about four kilos.

Sharks have twelve rows of teeth. The larger sharks can cut through a man's body in one bite, although they don't normally prey on humans.

Teeth are only one way to make food easy to swallow. Some spiders inject their prey with liquids, which turn the prey into a gooey mass.

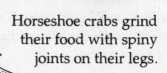

Horseshoe crabs grind their food with spiny joints on their legs.

GLUG

So now the mouthful of food is all squidgy and sloppy, it's time for a swallow and for the food to start its journey. A flap of skin, called the *epiglottis*, cuts off the breathing tubes (otherwise you'd choke to death on the first mouthful because the food would get into your lungs), and powerful muscles squidge the food down the throat. The muscles behind the food tighten and those in front relax in a sort of ripple effect, called *peristalsis*. This pushes the food ever further into the dark depths beneath.

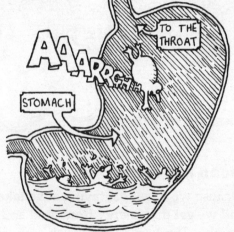

GURGLE

The stomach is a sort of waiting room for food. Water can pass through it in a few minutes, porridge may stay there for an hour and a mixed meal can hang around for up to two hours. But it's not a friendly waiting room. It's a slurping, burping lake of weak hydrochloric acid. Muscles in the stomach wall churn food and acid together into a creamy broth.

The remains of the food are squidged and squeezed

and bubbled and mixed with liquids that ooze out of the stomach wall. And the same thing happens all the way along the alimentary canal. These liquids help break down the food into all the different chemicals that it is made of, so that the body can take them in easily and use them. This is the process called *digestion*.

In the mood for food

We eat because we have to. Staying alive takes a lot of energy and we get that energy from food and from the air we breathe. The best food energy sources are fats and carbohydrates. (Carbohydrates are found in foods such as bread, potatoes and rice.)

THE ALIMENTARY CANAL - AND BEYOND

Now the remains of the food are reaching the end of their journey. By this time they contain the remains of bacteria which break down both food which cannot be used by the body and the cell walls of plants, known as *fibre*, which have little food value in themselves. Water is removed from the remains of the food in the last lengths of tube and returned to the body, but the fibre is so sodden with water that it keeps the rest of the waste soft and squidgy and therefore easy to squeeze out of the body as faeces 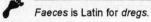 .

Constipation, being unable to get rid of faeces, used to be known as the 'English Disease' because people didn't eat enough fruit, vegetables and wholemeal bread and so didn't get enough fibre. Henry VIII had terrible problems because he hardly ate anything except meat.

YOUR POTTY, YOUR MAJESTY

WHAT'S THE POINT?

Faeces is Latin for *dregs*.

35

As for the bacteria: most of them are harmless while they're in the intestine, but they can make you ill if they get into your mouth or your throat. When you flush the toilet, millions of them get sprayed into the air in an invisible mist. They cover all surfaces including your face, your hands and your clothes. That's why it's important to close the toilet lid before you flush, and to wash your hands after.

Not all animals want to get rid of their waste products. Rhinoceroses build piles of dung to mark their territory, as do rabbits. If you keep a rabbit in the house, it's best to find out where it wants its dung-heap and then leave newspaper there. Just keep changing the newspaper - it's easier than cleaning up rabbit droppings all over the house!

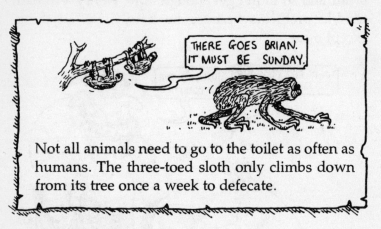

THERE GOES BRIAN. IT MUST BE SUNDAY.

Not all animals need to go to the toilet as often as humans. The three-toed sloth only climbs down from its tree once a week to defecate.

WASTE REMOVALS

All living things need to keep a constant level of water in their bodies. Kidneys remove excess fluid and some unwanted waste products from the blood. This liquid, or urine, flows down to the bladder, which can expand like a balloon and can take up to four hundred cubic centimetres before you have to go to the toilet. Interestingly, urine is clean when it first leaves the body. The Siberian Chukchi used to pass round a bucket after meals. Whoever wanted to could give their urine which the housewife then used to wash the table. They even dipped grass in it to wipe their face and hands!

AN ATHLETE'S ARMPIT

YOUR SKIN
- AND THE THINGS WHICH LIVE IN IT

All living things have some sort of skin which protects them from the outside world.

OUR LITTLE FRIENDS

As long as they stay on the surface of your skin, the bacteria from the toilet won't do you any harm. In fact they're in good company. On your skin is a creeping crawling mass of bacteria and other microbes - there are thousands of bacteria on every square centimetre, each one about two thousandths of a millimetre long. Some hide under dead flakes of skin, others dangle on thin strands of bacteria-stuff. There are at least three million on your face alone because they like the film of grease on your forehead. And they're specially fond of damp, dark places such as your armpits.

Most skin bacteria are your friends. They fight off unfriendly bacteria by oozing poisonous liquids, or by eating up all there is to eat in a circle round the enemy bacteria, so that they starve to death.

 Although there are billions of them, the bacteria inside and on the surface of an average human body are so small they could all fit into a teacup.

38

YOUR VERY OWN WATERPROOF BODY-STOCKING

Skin bacteria are useful but skin itself is vital. Like the first Fiona we are mostly made up of water - about seventy per cent of us is water. Without nice greasy skin the water would leak out and enemy bacteria would get in. Skin is much thicker and spongier than you might imagine: it weighs sixteen per cent of our total weight, and there are about two square metres of the stuff on an average adult.

KNOW YOUR SKIN

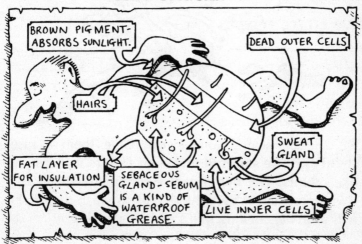

BROWN PIGMENT-ABSORBS SUNLIGHT.

DEAD OUTER CELLS

HAIRS

SWEAT GLAND

FAT LAYER FOR INSULATION

SEBACEOUS GLAND - SEBUM IS A KIND OF WATERPROOF GREASE.

LIVE INNER CELLS

BARE CONDITIONING

Our bodies have to stay at about the same temperature all the time. Get too hot or too cold and we die. But it's not easy to keep our bodies at the same temperature: one minute we may be out throwing snow balls, the next we may be in by a nice hot fire.

In fact we get hot just living - our cells produce heat as they burn up energy from food. And if we're ill, we often get hotter while our bodies try to fight off the illness - that's why you may have your temperature taken with a thermometer to see how ill you are. It's a real problem staying the same temperature - call in the sweat glands!

We have sweat glands all over our skin. Whenever we get too hot, for instance after exercise, these glands ooze out salty water. The water then dries on the skin and this has the effect of cooling us down.

Of course bacteria love sweat. Give them a nice, sweaty athlete's armpit and soon they're multiplying like rabbits. The bacteria give off smelly gases as a waste product. If the athlete fails to wash, he or she will soon be smelling like a rabbit as well.

HAIR CONDITIONING

Sometimes your body gets too cold. Then you may shiver. Shivering makes your muscles work and warms you up as exercise does. Or you may get goose-pimples ...

You've probably noticed that people are less furry than gorillas. We have clothes to keep us warm. But look closely at your skin: except your eyeballs, the palms of your hands and the soles of your feet, you're covered in tiny hairs. This is your fur - what there is of it. Once upon a time our ancestors had fur just as gorillas do, and when we got cold we would puff it out. This would trap more air between the hairs and the extra air would help to stop our body-heat from escaping. Furry animals still do this if they're cold - and so do we. Goose-pimples is your 'fur' standing on end.

Apart from the hair on your head, your body hair is probably very fine and short. But adults, and especially a lot of adult men, have quite a lot of it.

A MAN IN HIS NATURAL STATE

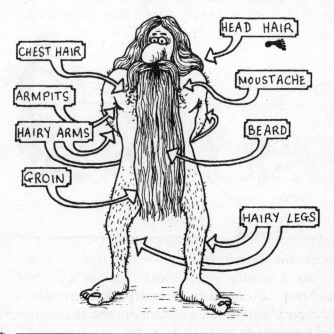

 Redheads have about 170,000 hairs on their heads, dark-haired people have around 200,000. Fair-haired people have something in between.

The fur on many animals is very dense, so dense that even water cannot penetrate to the skin. For instance, the fur of the Australian duck-billed platypus is thin and woolly near the root, but flattened and spear-shaped at the tip. This helps the platypus to keep warm, while at the same time creating a streamlined surface for swimming.

Hair grows from your skin like rope. At the base of each hair is a gland which smears grease on to it. So if you've got long hair you've got long greasy ropes of cells sticking out of your head. It's like walking around with sticky fly-paper instead of a hat: you pick up most bits of dirt and dust that are going. People with long hair would end up with a small bucket's worth of muck in it every year if they never washed or brushed it.

A YEAR'S DIRT

As for the bacteria - a sweaty armpit is good, but a sweaty, hairy, greasy armpit is heaven. They can work up enough stink to make a skunk jealous if we give them the chance and don't wash.

DR DANDELION'S DATA DETAILS

Check out this summary of skin and what it does.

 All living things have some sort of skin.

 Your skin is crawling with millions of bacteria.

 Most skin bacteria are harmless.

 Skin keeps water in and germs out.

 Our bodies have to stay at the same temperature.

 Sweat cools us down.

STAND UP AND BE COUNTED

BAG OF SKIN SEEKS BONES AND MUSCLES TO STAND UP IN

BONE ALONE

So you've got enough to eat, you've got your skin on, you've got the right amount of water and you're at the right temperature. What else do you need?

Well, bones for a start. Without them you would be a shapeless sack of skin with slimy stuff inside. Bones, teeth and nails are the only unbendable things in our bodies. We couldn't stand up without bones to take the weight.

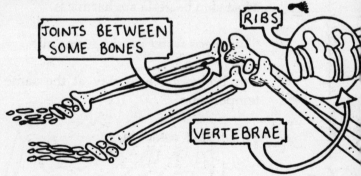

JOINTS BETWEEN SOME BONES

RIBS

VERTEBRAE

Remember the Bible story that Eve was created from Adam's rib? When the famous scientist Vesalius lectured on the Human Body in sixteenth century Padua, in Italy, he shocked his audience by showing that men and women have the same number of ribs, which meant the Bible must have been wrong.

The problem with bones is that they are *too* unbendable. If all your bones were joined up, you wouldn't be able to move.

That's why there are movable joints between some bones. Joints only allow you to move a bit - try bending your arm the wrong way at the elbow. Or rather DON'T - it could hurt. It's useful to do stretching exercises, to keep your joints in working order as you get older.

People have skeletons inside their bodies. So do fish, birds, snakes and frogs and a lot of other animals. But this is not the case with many simpler creatures. Animals such as insects and spiders have a hard, shell-like skeleton on the outside. Slugs and many other small creatures don't need a skeleton at all.

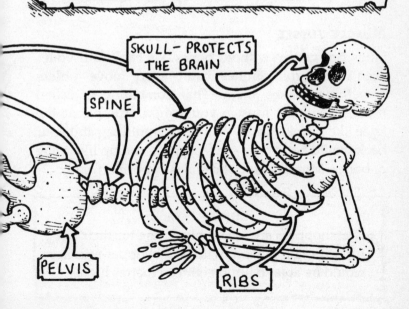

SKULL - PROTECTS THE BRAIN

SPINE

PELVIS

RIBS

Sharks only have bendy bones made from cartilage, the same sort of stuff your ears are made of.

MUSCLE TUSSLE

Slugs can get by without bones, we can't. But bones aren't enough - bones can't even move unless something makes them. That something is called muscle. Without muscle you would crumple at the knee like a broken doll, your head would sag and your back would bend over - in fact you'd end up like a bag of bones. Muscles hold the bones in position.

MUSCLE FACT
Grasshoppers are incredibly strong for their size. An average person with grasshopper-muscles would be able to jump eighteen metres high.

Muscles are clumps of cells which can shorten or lengthen, a bit like elastic bands. They're attached to bones by tendons, which pull on the the bones and make them move when the muscles change length.

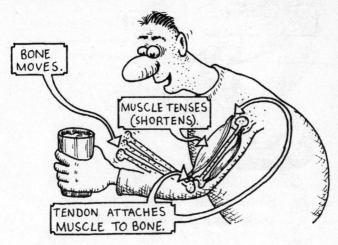

But why should a muscle want to shorten? It's probably quite happy just lying there doing nothing.

There are two types of muscle systems. One lot are designed to keep working whether you want them to or not - that goes for the muscles which make your heart pump and your alimentary canal squidge. The other lot, for instance the muscles which move your arms and legs, only work when nerve messages from your brain tell them to .

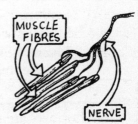

 Not quite always. In *reflex* actions, for instance blinking if something comes near the eye suddenly, the muscles work without a message from the brain telling them to.

DR DANDELION'S DATA DETAILS

Check out this summary of bones and muscles.

 Some animals, such as humans, have skeletons inside their bodies.

 Other animals, such as insects, have skeletons outside their bodies.

 The joints between bones allow for movement.

 Muscles are attached to bones by tendons.

 Muscles work by shortening and lengthening.

TAKE A DEEP BREATH!

WHY YOU BREATHE AND WHAT BLOOD DOES

A WELL SLUNG LUNG

Most living things need air. Most animals which have bones, including humans, get it through two big spongy things called *lungs*, beneath their ribs ◀. In humans the lungs are made up of between ten and twenty million tiny little tubes. When you breathe you suck air into them. Air is a mixture of gases and what you're after is not air as such, it's the *oxygen* in the air.

A muscle without oxygen is just a lump of meat. It's useless - unless you eat it! It needs oxygen in order to burn the fuel which makes it work. This fuel is called *glucose*, a type of sugar, and comes from food. Oxygen and glucose are both carried to the muscles by blood.

 Insects don't have lungs. They take in oxygen through many tiny holes in their skin.

DON'T HOLD YOUR BREATH!

You've probably noticed that if you breathe in and hold your breath for up to a minute, your limbs start to feel tired. This is because your body is running out of oxygen.

It's dangerous to hold your breath too long. If you do, you will go unconscious. There are also long term dangers if you do it too often. Pearl divers, who train themselves to stay under water for several minutes while they hunt for pearls in oyster shells, end up looking old before their time.

Whales and dolphins don't have that problem. Although they are not fish, but mammals like us, they are specially built for living in the sea and can stay under water without breathing for long periods. The sperm whale can dive as deep as three thousand metres, and stay there for nearly two hours!

THE STORY OF OXYGEN

Long, long ago, when the Earth was young, there was almost no free oxygen in the air. For millions of years all creatures had to get their energy from food, without breathing in oxygen. Then along came plants which give off free oxygen as part of their life processes. Millions more years passed, until finally the air was rich with lovely, sweet, breathable oxygen from plants, ready for animals like us to breathe.

Much of what we breathe today is incredibly ancient. We don't use up all the oxygen in each breath - about a sixth of it is breathed out again. The amazing thing is how the unused oxygen spreads out and mixes with the rest of the air in the world. You can be pretty certain that in every breath you breathe are bits of oxygen from almost every breath that anyone ever took in the last two thousand years.

A DAY IN THE LIFE OF A BIT OF BLOOD

The journey of blood round the body is called *circulation*.

With each breath, oxygen passes through the very thin walls of the tubes in our lungs and is then whisked away in the blood, which rushes along tiny blood-tubes, or capillaries as they are known, beside the lung tubes.

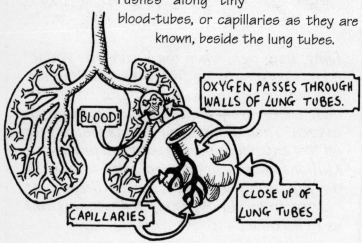

OXYGEN PASSES THROUGH WALLS OF LUNG TUBES.

BLOOD

CLOSE UP OF LUNG TUBES

CAPILLARIES

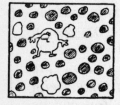

Blood is a soup of red and white cells which float in a liquid called plasma. The oxygen is absorbed by the red cells. In fact it's oxygen which makes them a nice bright red: without it they're more of a dark, purply-red colour.

The oxygen-rich blood rushes off to the heart along a large tube called the pulmonary vein.

GURGLE

The heart pumps oxygen-poor blood back to the lungs. On average it takes forty-five seconds for a drop of blood to complete one whole circuit.

The heart pumps the oxygen-rich blood all over the body along arteries. The only arteries to carry de-oxygenated blood are the pulmonary arteries

Purply-red oxygen-poor blood returns to the heart along veins, carrying with it waste products from the cells including carbon dioxide gas which will soon be breathed out from the lungs.

Red blood cells deliver their oxygen to the muscles and to any other cells which need it. At the same time glucose from the digestive system is also delivered, along with other nutrients needed by the body.

The blood in the arteries is under pressure. Cut an artery and the blood can squirt out over three metres. You won't have long to live.

Brave Heart

Your heart muscle has to keep on beating from the moment you are born until the moment you die. It can never take a rest.

It has four chambers - two atriums and two ventricles.

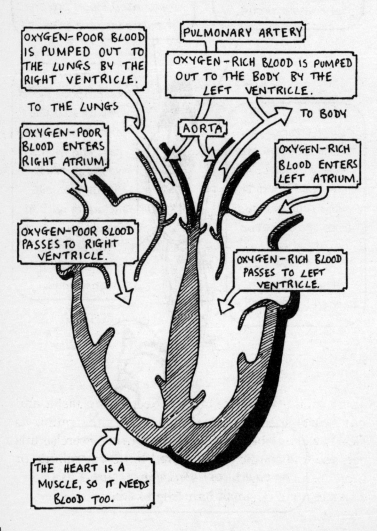

OXYGEN-POOR BLOOD IS PUMPED OUT TO THE LUNGS BY THE RIGHT VENTRICLE.

PULMONARY ARTERY

OXYGEN-RICH BLOOD IS PUMPED OUT TO THE BODY BY THE LEFT VENTRICLE.

TO THE LUNGS

AORTA

TO BODY

OXYGEN-POOR BLOOD ENTERS RIGHT ATRIUM.

OXYGEN-RICH BLOOD ENTERS LEFT ATRIUM.

OXYGEN-POOR BLOOD PASSES TO RIGHT VENTRICLE.

OXYGEN-RICH BLOOD PASSES TO LEFT VENTRICLE.

THE HEART IS A MUSCLE, SO IT NEEDS BLOOD TOO.

KEEP FIT

During exercise, our muscles suck up fuel as fast as we can feed it to them. Desperate for energy they scream for fuel.

To provide the fuel we breathe deeper and faster and our hearts speed up. A resting heart may pump as slowly as sixty beats per minute. During exercise this can rise to a frantic one hundred beats per minute or more, sending the blood swooshing round the body and feeding oxygen and glucose to where it's needed.

When exercise is over we may feel shattered for a few minutes, but after that we usually feel great. Exercise is the best medicine in the world. Here's what it does for you:

Exercise helps to keep your arteries free of fats. These fats can build up in the arteries which supply blood to the heart until an artery may become completely blocked. The heart is starved of blood, and it stops pumping. This is known as a heart attack.

Exercise strengthens and enlarges the heart muscle so that you're less likely to get a heart attack later in life.

Exercise helps you to fight diseases by strengthening your body's defence systems.

Exercise strengthens the muscles.

DR DANDELION'S DATA DETAILS

Check out this summary of blood and breathing.

♥ We breathe oxygen into our lungs.

♥ Oxygen burns glucose in our muscles to create energy.

♥ Oxygen is carried to the muscles in red blood cells.

♥ The heart pumps blood round the body.

♥ The system of heart, blood and lungs is called the circulatory system.

♥ Exercise strengthens the muscles and the circulatory system.

OFF SICK!

ILLNESSES AND HOW WE FIGHT THEM OFF

All living things can get ill, and we all have ways of fighting off disease. In humans, skin keeps most of the things which cause disease from getting into our bodies. But dangerous bugs, known as *germs* 🐾 or micro-organisms because they're so tiny, can still find a way in through wounds or when you eat or breathe. It helps to be fit when they strike, because your body, and especially your blood, has to work hard to fight them off.

THE FIRST LINES OF DEFENCE

SNOT

Tiny mucus-covered 🐾 hairs in your nose and lungs capture specks of germ-laden dirt from the air you breathe. The dirty mucus comes out of your nose when you blow it or is swallowed.

VOMIT
The stomach walls clench in a violent spasm, forcing bad or poisonous food and drink out of your mouth.

 This comes from the Latin word *germen* meaning either a sprout or a tiny creature in its mother's womb.

🐾🐾 *Mucus* is a sort of sticky slime.

58

COUGH

A cough forces dirty mucus out of your throat and lungs.

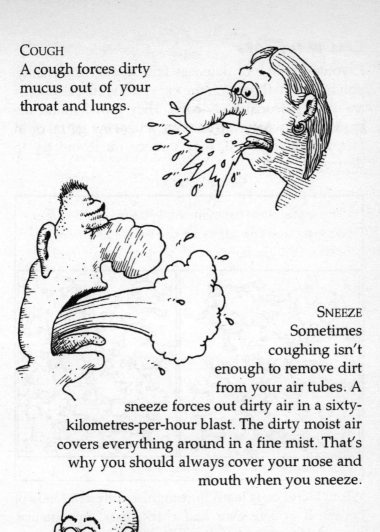

SNEEZE

Sometimes coughing isn't enough to remove dirt from your air tubes. A sneeze forces out dirty air in a sixty-kilometres-per-hour blast. The dirty moist air covers everything around in a fine mist. That's why you should always cover your nose and mouth when you sneeze.

EAR WAX

Ear wax comes from special sweat glands. It's sticky and it traps dirt before the dirt goes too deep into your ears.

CALL IN THE COPS

If your first line of defences fails to stop the enemy, you have to fall back on the experts. White blood cells are your personal body-cops. They prowl round the system and whenever they see an enemy germ, or in fact any strange cell, they pounce on it and try to destroy it.

GERM WARFARE

The white blood cells on the left are able to catch and destroy the germs on the right - all except one germ. Can you work out which germ will go free?

Answer. The one with the square on its head.

White blood cells learn to recognise different kinds of germs. If you've ever had chickenpox for instance, your white blood cells will have learnt how to recognise and kill chickenpox bugs. So if ever chickenpox bugs get in your body again, the white cells can destroy them quickly before they take hold. In other words, you are *immune* to the illness.

Nowadays it's possible to become immune to many illnesses without actually catching them. This is what

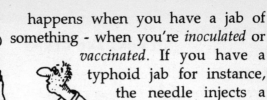

happens when you have a jab of something - when you're *inoculated* or *vaccinated*. If you have a typhoid jab for instance, the needle injects a weakened version of the typhoid germs so that your white blood cells learn to recognise active typhoid bacteria should they ever try to infect you for real.

WORM GERMS

Our defences are very strong, but sometimes the enemy overwhelms them. Then the germs will start to multiply rapidly. That's when you get seriously ill, and that's when you may have to call for a doctor.

The germs which cause illness are so incredibly small that they cannot be seen without a microscope - and microscopes only became useful around 1677 when a Dutchman called Anton van Leeuwenhoek built one strong enough to see *micro-organisms* . Until just over a hundred years ago there were all kinds of strange ideas about what caused illnesses.

 A micro-organism or microbe is a living thing which can only be seen with the aid of a microscope.

DEMONS AND GERMS

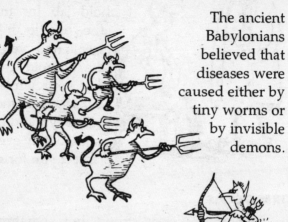

The ancient Babylonians believed that diseases were caused either by tiny worms or by invisible demons.

The Saxons believed that elves shot darts of pain and illness into people. (They believed in the germ-worms as well.)

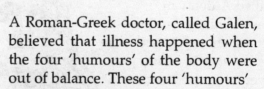

A Roman-Greek doctor, called Galen, believed that illness happened when the four 'humours' of the body were out of balance. These four 'humours' were black bile, phlegm, yellow bile and blood.

Leeuwenhoek, the Dutchman, made more than four hundred microscope lenses during his life. Some of the lenses were no bigger than the head of a pin, but with them he spotted the tiny wriggling 'vermicules' which we now know as bacteria - the Babylonian idea of horrible worms wasn't so mad after all.

VICIOUS VIRUSES

But Leeuwenhoek was never able to see the smallest germs of all. These are the viruses. They're so small and strange that compared to most of them an average bacterium is the size of a house.

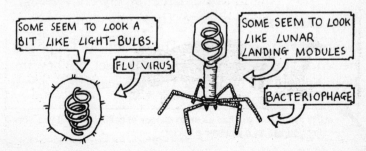

SOME SEEM TO LOOK A BIT LIKE LIGHT-BULBS.

FLU VIRUS

SOME SEEM TO LOOK LIKE LUNAR LANDING MODULES

BACTERIOPHAGE

STOP!

Most scientists think that viruses are alive, but it's hard to decide. They can only reproduce by invading the cells of living creatures and using those cells to help them reproduce. All other living things reproduce using only their own cells.

Colds, flu, measles and chickenpox are all caused by viruses. And, unfortunately, new viruses are turning up all the time. If one of them attacks you, you could be in serious trouble. It's hard for scientists to create new medicines to kill new viruses without killing you as well, because enemy viruses make their home *inside* your cells .

That's why illnesses caused by bacteria are often easier to treat, because the bacteria don't actually get inside your cells.

THE LAST RESORT

Suppose you're really sick. The doctor can't cope , he sends you to hospital. Sounds perfect, but beware - hospitals are full of diseased people - and their germs.

Until the 1920s, you had as much chance of getting better if you looked after yourself as if you saw a doctor.

THE SAD STORY OF SEMMELWEISS

Hospitals must be kept incredibly clean or germs will get everywhere.

The ancient Egyptians and Greeks understood about cleanliness. Egyptian priest-doctors used to bathe four times a day and shave off all their body hair. Doctors like the Greek, Hippocrates (called the 'Father of Medicine') treated their sick in temples which were kept spotless. Then the idea of clean hospitals got lost. European hospitals became disgustingly dirty and many patients used to die.

In the nineteenth century a Hungarian doctor, Ignaz Semmelweis, made the doctors under him wash their hands in disinfectant to kill germs, but the doctors forced him to leave his hospital. They did not believe that the disinfectants worked. Later Semmelweis got septicaemia (blood-poisoning) in a finger and died - from the very type of disease he had tried to stop.

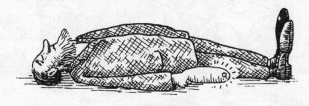

Cleanliness is specially important if you're in hospital for an operation. It's easy to understand why: a deep cut in your skin is a major hole in your personal body-armour.

In the past, your chances of living after an operation were pretty slim. Surgeons used dirty saws or knives, then enemy bugs would breed in the warm damp depths of the dirty cut. This meant the wound went rotten. Soon it started to smell and the rot spread. Then you either went rotten and died - or they chopped the rotten bit off. Nowadays, however, if you go rotten you can be treated with antibiotics.

DR DANDELION'S DATA DETAILS

Check out this summary of illness, and how to fight it off.

Illnesses are caused by germs.

Germs are either bacteria or viruses.

White blood cells destroy germs.

White blood cells can learn to recognise the germs which cause an illness, so making you immune to it.

Vacination or inoculation gives immunity to some illnesses.

Baby Boom!

Having babies
– and looking after them

Nearly all living things are able to reproduce themselves.

Too many babies

Some creatures have a few babies and look after them, some have lots and don't.

The female cod lays about seven million eggs at one time. It's enough if only seven out of seven million grow up to have babies of their own. Seven per mother and the race of cod should go on for ever - well, almost.

THINGS ARE A BIT FISHY, IF YOU ASK ME.

IF ONLY WE HAD SOME CHIPS.

Cod produce a lot of babies, and most of them get eaten by other animals. It's a good thing they do, or the whole Earth would soon be awash with large fish. And the danger of being squashed by cod would be as nothing compared with the danger of being smothered in bacteria, if bacteria didn't die off. Bacteria don't have mums and dads; they just split in two like Fiona. Given the right conditions, they can do this every twenty minutes. That means that if all the descendants of one bacterium could survive and divide, they would weigh more than the Sun and all its planets within a week!

MUMS, DADS AND THINGS IN BETWEEN

There are two main ways of reproducing. Creatures which are neither male nor female just divide in two like most bacteria do. This is called *asexual reproduction*. The other method is *sexual reproduction*, when both a male and a female parent are needed to produce a new life which is a mixture of both of them.

Bacterium is singular. *Bacteria* is plural. So you have *one* bacterium, but *two or more* bacteria.

Most kinds of plants and animals have males and females and make babies by sexual reproduction.

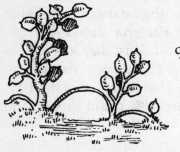

Most micro-organisms and quite a lot of plants do it on their own. This is called asexual reproduction.

Some plants and animals, such as earthworms, are both male and female at the same time. And some of them can reproduce by both sexual or asexual methods.

YOU AND YOUR EGG

Women have eggs, but unlike hens they don't lay them. This is because people are a type of animal called *mammals*. Mammal babies develop inside their mothers where they are safe and protected. After the babies are born, their mothers feed them milk from their *mammary glands* (the scientific word for breasts).

One small group of mammals, called monotremes, lay eggs. The Australian duck-billed platypus is one of these. The young still feed on milk after they hatch.

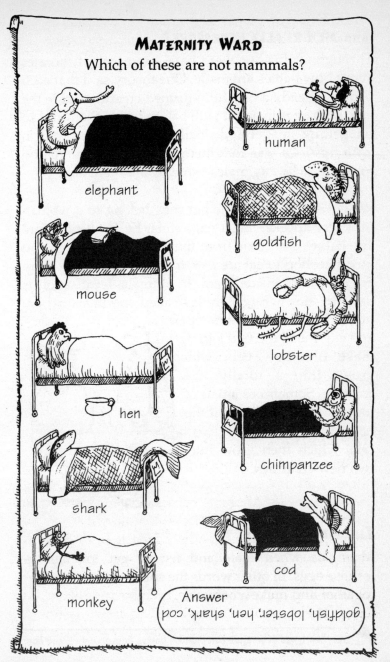

MATERNITY WARD
Which of these are not mammals?

elephant

human

mouse

goldfish

hen

lobster

shark

chimpanzee

monkey

cod

Answer
goldfish, lobster, hen, shark, cod

ARE MEN REALLY NECESSARY?

Throughout history there have been lots of theories about how babies are made. One theory said that each baby is already a tiny fully-formed creature inside the egg, with eggs inside it with babies inside them and so on, getting smaller and smaller for ever. The problem with this idea was that there seemed to be no reason for there to be any males - so why are there any?

We now know that whether they belong to a woman or a woodpecker most eggs must be *fertilised* before any babies can come from them . The eggs you buy in a shop to eat are *unfertilised* which is why there are no chicks inside them. In animals, fertilisation is done by tiny wriggly things called sperm which are made by males. When sperm and egg meet, the two join up to make one new cell, which grows into a totally new creature. Sometimes a pair of identical twins is made, if the new cell divides into two cells which then grow into two new creatures.

THE MATING GAME

Mating is when male and female get together to fertilise eggs. In other words the sperm and the egg get together and make a baby.

Very few types of creature can produce babies from an unfertilised egg.

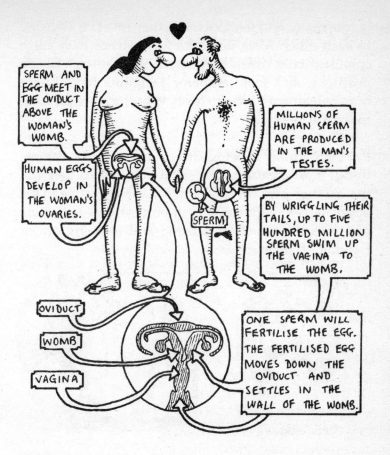

SPERM AND EGG MEET IN THE OVIDUCT ABOVE THE WOMAN'S WOMB.

HUMAN EGGS DEVELOP IN THE WOMAN'S OVARIES.

MILLIONS OF HUMAN SPERM ARE PRODUCED IN THE MAN'S TESTES.

SPERM

BY WRIGGLING THEIR TAILS, UP TO FIVE HUNDRED MILLION SPERM SWIM UP THE VAGINA TO THE WOMB.

OVIDUCT

WOMB

VAGINA

ONE SPERM WILL FERTILISE THE EGG. THE FERTILISED EGG MOVES DOWN THE OVIDUCT AND SETTLES IN THE WALL OF THE WOMB.

The new creature is a mixture of what its parents are. In other words, it gets its *characteristics* from both of them. This is why a brown-eyed, dark-haired man and a blue-eyed, blond woman may produce a brown-eyed, blond baby or a blue-eyed, dark-haired baby, and so on - and why you probably look a bit like your father as well as your mother.

 Leeuwenhoek, who by using his microscope was the first person to see human sperm, thought that the head of each one contained a tiny human being.

Before males and females mate, they must be attracted to each other. Male peacocks for instance have huge colourful tails which they show off to attract female peacocks, and male emperor penguins have bright orange feathers on their chests which are pleasing to female penguins.

But there's more to being attractive than looks. For one thing, most creatures can smell better than they can see. So they give off smells which are attractive to the opposite sex. Behaviour is important too. For many creatures this involves dancing and showing off, or fighting off male rivals.

Dancing is a way of showing off.

There are many other ways of attracting a mate. Here are just three examples:

The bower bird builds a beautiful nest in order to attract a female.

 In one unkind experiment on sexual attraction, the orange patches of a group of male penguins were painted over. The poor males never managed to get any females.

74

Young girls in some
Siberian tribes used to
collect lice to throw at the
young men they wanted
to marry.

Fireworms float to the
surface of the Pacific Ocean fifty-five
minutes after sunset, once a month when the moon is
in its third quarter. Then the females start to glow with
light and the males flash on and off in reply.

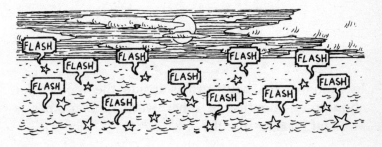

IT'S A BABY!

An egg, or *ovum* , is a single cell. Once fertilised
the cell divides in two then those cells divide, and so
on again and again, so that each time the cells divide,
the egg is twice as big as it was before.

Ovum means the female cell which joins with the male sperm cell in all
sexually reproducing living things. It comes from the Latin for egg. The
word *egg* in English can mean either an ovum, or just an egg such as a
fish's or bird's egg.

Soon the cells start to specialise. Some become muscle cells, some bone and so on. Pretty soon, although the group of cells is only a few centimetres long, it starts to look like a tiny creature. This tiny creature is called a *foetus*.

The human foetus depends on its mother for everything. Mother is supermarket, chemist, sewage works, swimming pool and bedroom all rolled into one. She delivers food and oxygen and everything the foetus needs down a tube called the *umbilical cord*, while waste products from the baby are removed up the same tube .

In humans, the baby grows inside the mother for about nine months, in other words the mother is *pregnant* for nine months.

After nine months the baby is born and breathes air, using its lungs for the first time. It no longer needs the umbilical cord which is now cut and tied. The bit attached to the baby shrivels away, and this ends up as your belly-button or *navel* .

In the past, people thought that anything that happened to the mother could affect the baby. In 1726 a Guildford woman who was frightened by a rabbit while pregnant, said she had given birth to a litter of rabbits.

In the Middle Ages there used to be a big argument about whether Adam and Eve had navels, given that they didn't have a mother.

A PREGANT PAUSE

The mouse opossum of South and Central America gives birth to what are probably the smallest of all mammal  babies - some are only as big as a grain of wheat. The pregnancy of an opossum mother only lasts for thirteen days, or less.

At the other end of the scale, the female Indian elephant has a pregnancy of over twenty months. But then, her baby is a *lot* bigger!

The prize for the biggest baby has to go to the blue whale. The female is pregnant for a mere eleven months, but her new-born calf weighs up to two tonnes and can be over seven metres long.

The most fertile mammal must be the meadow vole. Female voles are ready to start breeding at twenty-five days old, and they can have litters of up to eight babies up to seventeen times a year. That's 136 babies a year, if they're lucky!

One of these babies is not a baby- which one is it?

Answer. The one with horns is a demon.

Very young babies still depend on their mothers for almost everything. They get all the food they need from their mother's milk, or from bottled milk if that's not possible. And they have a lovely lazy time in most cases. All they have to do is cry a bit and then they can suck up all the food they want, almost without moving!

But gradually they have to switch over to solid food. This process is called *weaning*. Young creatures need a lot of food in order to grow, and milk on its own is not enough.

Many creatures, such as many baby fish, never get any help from their mothers. The female lays her unfertilised eggs outside her body and the male comes along afterwards to release his sperm over them. As soon as the babies hatch out they are able to swim off and look after themselves. Some fish are not caring parents.

Mammal babies take longer to grow into adults than simpler animals such as fish. Human children need their parents to look after them for years before the children are ready to look after themselves.

GROWING UP

Human children look pretty much like adult humans from the time they are born - although there are some changes.

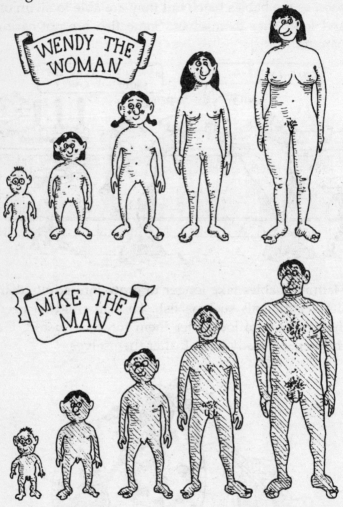

WENDY THE WOMAN

MIKE THE MAN

Children are lucky. They have soft stretchy skin: when they grow, their skin grows with them.

A human child looks roughly like a human adult, but many creatures change so much that you wouldn't know that there was any connection between the young form and the adult form just by looking at them. Pity poor insects. Because they have hard skeletons on the outside of their bodies, many of them have to keep shedding their outer layers as they grow bigger. New, soft outer skeletons form underneath the old ones. Then the old one cracks off and the new skeleton hardens once it is uncovered. But the insect is unprotected and at great risk until the new skeleton is hard.

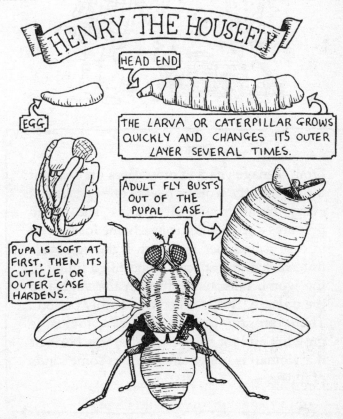

HENRY THE HOUSEFLY

HEAD END

EGG

THE LARVA OR CATERPILLAR GROWS QUICKLY AND CHANGES ITS OUTER LAYER SEVERAL TIMES.

ADULT FLY BUSTS OUT OF THE PUPAL CASE.

PUPA IS SOFT AT FIRST, THEN ITS CUTICLE, OR OUTER CASE HARDENS.

TEENAGERS AND BEYOND

Some of the biggest changes in young humans take place at *puberty* which normally happens between the ages of eleven and seventeen, usually starting a little earlier in girls than in boys. Puberty is when the body reaches its adult form. After puberty, young humans are able to make babies of their own.

PERIODS

From teenage years in most cases up to about the age of fifty, women release one egg almost every month from their ovaries. The womb prepares a special lining as a home for the egg in case it becomes fertilised. If the egg stays unfertilised, the special blood-filled lining of the womb falls away through the vagina to the outside. This is called a 'monthly period'. There are no periods while a foetus is growing and for some time after it is born, or if a woman is under stress or has some kinds of illnesses.

GROWING DOWN

Most people are fully grown by the ages of seventeen to twenty. But almost as soon as they finish growing, they start to die. This is partly because our bodies fail to grow enough new cells to replace old cells when they die off. To begin with, they die so slowly it doesn't matter, even though people in their twenties are already losing a few thousand brain cells every day. In later years the dying speeds up - muscles get smaller, skin gets thinner, hair falls out or grows in unwanted places.

Then, perhaps seventy or eighty years after the sperm first met the egg, it's all over and you're dead.

And a good thing too. After all if people didn't die, soon the world would be chock-a-block with them and there wouldn't be room for any other creatures.

FAMILY MATTERS

ALL ABOUT EVOLUTION AND HOW PEOPLE AND CHIPMUNKS ARE RELATED

MY DARLING SPINACH

Why can't a mouse mate with a warthog? What's the matter with mousehogs? Or to go further: why can't spinach mate with a tiger? A plate of spingers might be very tasty.

The answer is that these different types of living things belong to different *species*. Members of each species can only produce 'babies which can have babies' if they mate with other members of the same species. That is to say, even if a mousehog was possible it would never be able to have any baby mousehogs .

In fact there are a few animals like mousehogs. The mule is a cross between a horse and a donkey, and mules can't have babies. The same goes for tigrons, which are a cross between a lion and a tiger.

IMPOSSIBLE ANIMALS

None of these cross-bred creatures is possible.
Can you guess what animals they came from?

Answers
1. Bumble-pig (half pig, half bumblebee) 2.
Crowkey (half crow, half monkey) 3. Leomouse
(half leopard, half mouse) 4. Osdog (half ostrich,
half dog) 5. Elerat (half elephant, half rat)

EVOLUTION

According to the Bible , God made all living things on the fifth and sixth day after he created the universe, and he made each species exactly as we see it today. The problem with this idea is that the species should stay as they are for ever, which is not what scientists think is really happening.

What scientists think is that some species die out and new species take their place.

How else to explain *fossils*? Fossils are the stony remains of ancient creatures. Fossil dinosaur bones are clearly the remains of a whole world of animals which has gone. But there are no fossils of humans among the fossils of dinosaurs, so dinosaurs must have died out before humans came along. And there were lots of other creatures in the meantime.

Evolution is the idea that new species evolve from old ones rather than being suddenly created brand-new by God. The idea as we know it today comes from Charles Darwin, a very great scientist, who came up with the idea of *natural selection*.

Calculating from the Bible, James Ussher, Archbishop of Armagh 1625-56, set the year for the creation of the world at exactly 4004 BC - about 4,500,000 years wrong!

DARWIN'S BIG IDEA:

An animal or a plant which fails to have babies will not pass on any of its characteristics to its children. Suppose a rabbit has short ears and poor hearing and a fox sneaks up behind it and catches it. And suppose this happens before the poor rabbit has had time to have any babies. The rabbit won't pass on its short ears to its children, and there will be fewer baby rabbits with short ears in the future.

Now suppose the rabbit's sister has long ears and good hearing. She can hear a fox coming up behind, no problem. This rabbit has a better chance of living long enough to have babies, and the babies may well have their mother's ears. Nature has *selected* the long-eared rabbits over the short-eared ones.

Of course not everything that gets passed on is the longest or the biggest. It depends what a species is good at. Mice may get better and better at running into mouseholes, while cats get better at pouncing on them. What survives may not be recognisable as the same species in thousands of years - mice may have survived which have evolved to look like cats!

NEW SPECIES

Darwin suggested that new species are developing all the time. Your gerbil, if you've got one, could be the ancestor of a species of giant elephant-gerbils which will rule the world in ten million years' time.

This is how a new species might develop.

First, imagine a group of people. Some of them have long noses and are good at sniffing out mushrooms.

Next, put the group on an island where there are lots of mushrooms and not much else and leave them there for a long time.

Come back in a few hundred thousand years and build a bridge to the island so that your group can meet up again with the rest of the human race.

The chances are that they will have evolved into a new species of mushroom-sniffers. They won't be able to mate with humans to make 'babies which can have babies' any more - they're a different species.

LONG FINGERS FOR GRUBBING UP MUSHROOMS

NOT MANY TEETH BECAUSE MUSHROOMS DON'T NEED TO BE CHEWED

NOSES FOR SNIFFING MUSHROOMS

PADDED KNEES FOR KNEELING ON

How new species develop was one of Darwin's big discoveries. Except he found out by looking at finches in the Galapagos Islands off South America.

EXTINCTION

We now know that all the millions of species of plants and animals which live on Earth today are only a tiny part of all the species which have lived in the past. The dead species, like the dinosaurs, are *extinct*.

When the last of the dinosaurs died out sixty-five million years ago, more than three quarters of all the other animal species alive at that time died out with them . In just the last 250 million years there have been up to twelve mass extinctions as well as lots of single species dying out on their own.

This has been calculated at 0.1%.

One theory is that giant rocks landing from outer space every few million years, called meteors, throw up dust. The dust blots out the Sun, without sunlight the Earth freezes over, and this causes mass extinctions such as the one which finished the dinosaurs. Another theory is that dinosaurs died of constipation when flowering plants came along - flowering plants didn't give them enough fibre. But this theory doesn't explain how all the other species died out.

Your family tree

All modern humans belong to the same species. The differences between different races, such as hair and skin colour, are mostly on the surface. Underneath we're all pretty much the same. Many scientists now think that our species is descended from a single woman whom they have named Eve, after the Eve in the Bible. This Eve probably lived in Africa about two hundred thousand years ago.

Going further back, humans and apes are probably descended from a common chimpanzee-like ancestor, called Proconsul by the scientists, which lived ten to twenty million years ago. Her descendants evolved in different ways.

Further back still, we share a common ancestor with all other mammals, which looked a bit like a shrew.

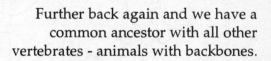

Further back again and we have a common ancestor with all other vertebrates - animals with backbones.

And of course going right back to the beginning, in the blob of chemicals we called Fiona, we share a common ancestor with all living things.

You and your relatives

Scientists have found ways of grouping, or *categorising*, all living things to show how they are related to each other. The groups may be based on physical characteristics, such as the the shape of bones. They're meant to show how things are related to each other.

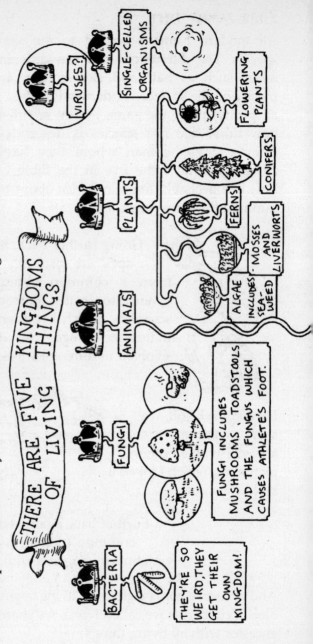

THERE ARE FIVE KINGDOMS OF LIVING THINGS

BACTERIA

THEY'RE SO WEIRD, THEY GET THEIR OWN KINGDOM!

FUNGI

FUNGI INCLUDES MUSHROOMS, TOADSTOOLS AND THE FUNGUS WHICH CAUSES ATHLETE'S FOOT.

ANIMALS

PLANTS

ALGAE INCLUDES SEA-WEED

MOSSES AND LIVERWORTS

FERNS

CONIFERS

FLOWERING PLANTS

VIRUSES?

SINGLE-CELLED ORGANISMS

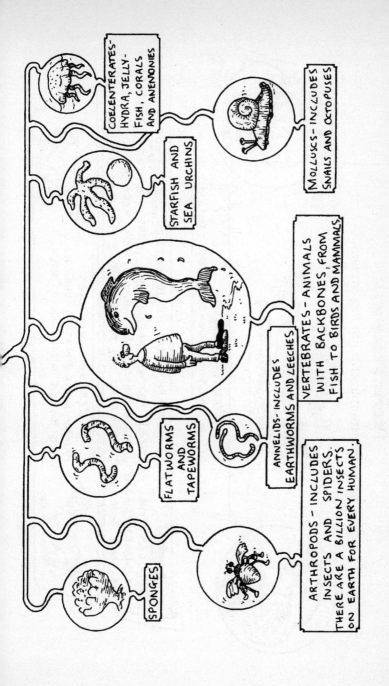

COELENTERATES - HYDRA, JELLY-FISH, CORALS AND ANEMONES

MOLLUSCS - INCLUDES SNAILS AND OCTOPUSES

STARFISH AND SEA URCHINS

VERTEBRATES - ANIMALS WITH BACKBONES, FROM FISH TO BIRDS AND MAMMALS

ANNELIDS - INCLUDES EARTHWORMS AND LEECHES

FLATWORMS AND TAPEWORMS

ARTHROPODS - INCLUDES INSECTS AND SPIDERS. THERE ARE A BILLION INSECTS ON EARTH FOR EVERY HUMAN.

SPONGES

93

People Pyramid

This is how humans fit into this system.

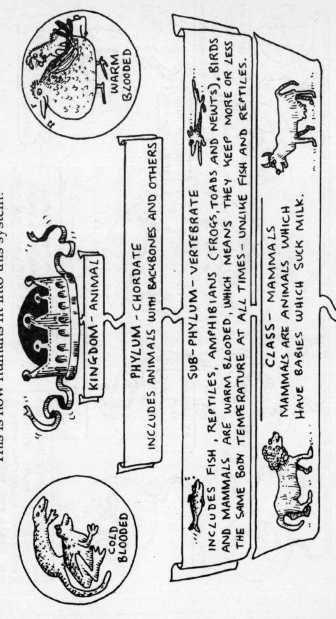

WARM BLOODED

COLD BLOODED

KINGDOM – ANIMAL

PHYLUM – CHORDATE
INCLUDES ANIMALS WITH BACKBONES AND OTHERS

SUB-PHYLUM – VERTEBRATE
INCLUDES FISH, REPTILES, AMPHIBIANS (FROGS, TOADS AND NEWTS), BIRDS AND MAMMALS ARE WARM BLOODED, WHICH MEANS THEY KEEP MORE OR LESS THE SAME BODY TEMPERATURE AT ALL TIMES – UNLIKE FISH AND REPTILES.

CLASS – MAMMALS
MAMMALS ARE ANIMALS WHICH HAVE BABIES WHICH SUCK MILK.

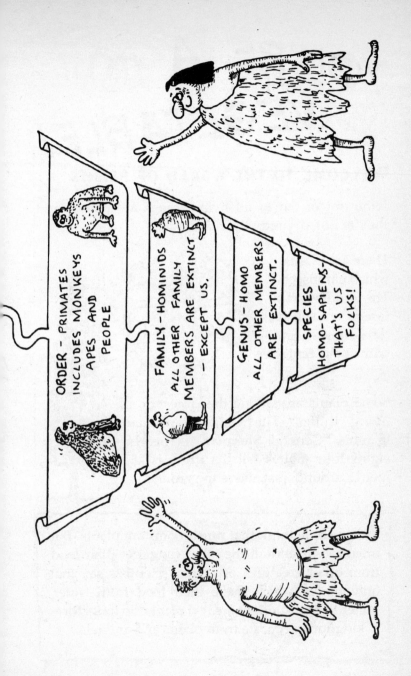

ORDER - PRIMATES INCLUDES MONKEYS APES AND PEOPLE

FAMILY - HOMINIDS ALL OTHER FAMILY MEMBERS ARE EXTINCT - EXCEPT US.

GENUS - HOMO ALL OTHER MEMBERS ARE EXTINCT.

SPECIES HOMO-SAPIENS- THAT'S US FOLKS!

YOU'RE A VEGETABLE!

WELCOME TO THE WORLD OF PLANTS

Nine out of ten of all living things are plants, and they're not all pretty little buttercups ...

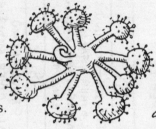

There are plants which eat insects. The Sundew traps insects on its leaves, then digests them with sticky tentacles.

Some plants are among the largest of all living things. The Californian Giant Sequoia 'General Sherman' is nearly eighty-four metres tall. Its trunk is 25.3 metres around, just above the ground.

Most people think that mushrooms are plants. But mushrooms and all the other fungi get their food from other creatures or plants; scientists say that only plants which make their food from water, minerals and sunlight are real plants. So fungi form a 'kingdom' separate from plants and animals.

SUNLIGHT FOOD FACTORY

Photosynthesis is what plants do to get their food. They soak up sunshine, absorbing energy from it in the stuff which makes their leaves look green, called *chlorophyll*, then they use the energy to power the food factory in their leaves.

INSIDE THE FOOD FACTORY

Plants need to burn sugar with oxygen to stay alive, like most living things.

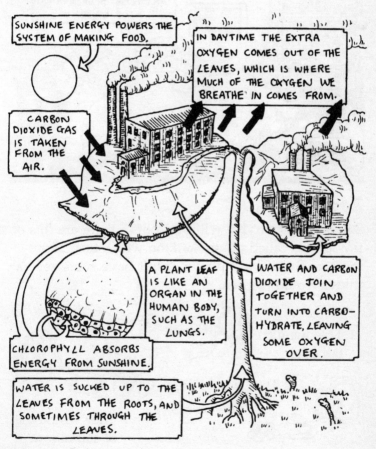

SUNSHINE ENERGY POWERS THE SYSTEM OF MAKING FOOD.

IN DAYTIME THE EXTRA OXYGEN COMES OUT OF THE LEAVES, WHICH IS WHERE MUCH OF THE OXYGEN WE BREATHE IN COMES FROM.

CARBON DIOXIDE GAS IS TAKEN FROM THE AIR.

A PLANT LEAF IS LIKE AN ORGAN IN THE HUMAN BODY, SUCH AS THE LUNGS.

WATER AND CARBON DIOXIDE JOIN TOGETHER AND TURN INTO CARBO-HYDRATE, LEAVING SOME OXYGEN OVER.

CHLOROPHYLL ABSORBS ENERGY FROM SUNSHINE.

WATER IS SUCKED UP TO THE LEAVES FROM THE ROOTS, AND SOMETIMES THROUGH THE LEAVES.

At night when there's no sunlight to give them energy, plants do not photosynthesise. Instead they use up their stores of sugar and have to absorb oxygen from the air in order to burn sugar, just as we do when we breathe. This is why plants are removed from hospital wards at night. Lucky for us that they 'breathe' out more oxygen in the day than they 'breathe' in at night.

Roots

Some plants survive without roots - there are lots of tiny plants called phytoplankton which float about in the sea. But if land plants didn't have roots several things would happen.

1. They would fall over.

2. They would die of thirst.

3. They would die of starvation.

Plants need their roots to take water and other vital chemicals from the soil. Water evaporates from the leaves and this causes a kind of 'suction', known as *transpiration*. The water and nutrients are 'pulled' up tiny tubes all the way from the roots to where they are needed. In tall trees, such as redwoods, transpiration can pull water over a hundred metres from the roots to the upper leaves. Other tiny tubes running alongside the transpiration tubes carry food from the leaves to other parts of the plant.

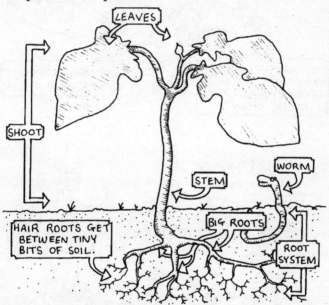

LONELY CABBAGE SEEKS CABBAGE FOR ROMANCE AND POSSIBLY BABY CABBAGES

Cabbages can have flowers, although you hardly ever see them because the poor cabbages get eaten before they have time to blossom. But if a cabbage does have flowers it may well be looking for a partner. Flowers are either male or female or both.

MRS FLOWER

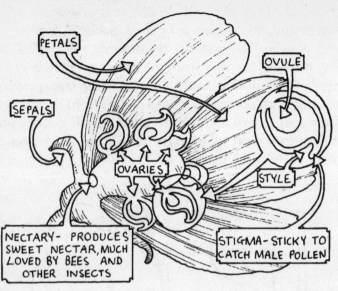

PETALS

SEPALS

OVULE

OVARIES

STYLE

NECTARY— PRODUCES SWEET NECTAR, MUCH LOVED BY BEES AND OTHER INSECTS

STIGMA— STICKY TO CATCH MALE POLLEN

MR FLOWER

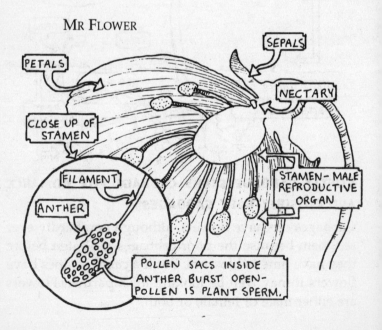

PETALS

SEPALS

NECTARY

CLOSE UP OF STAMEN

FILAMENT

ANTHER

STAMEN— MALE REPRODUCTIVE ORGAN

POLLEN SACS INSIDE ANTHER BURST OPEN— POLLEN IS PLANT SPERM.

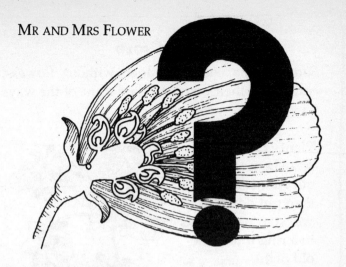

BEE OFF WITH YOU!

Pollen is mostly carried from the stamen of one flower
to the style of another flower on the wind or on insects,
best known of which is the busy bee.

This is how it works:
When a bee buzzes up to collect nectar (for making
honey) from inside a flower, pollen gets brushed off
the stamen on to its legs. Then having sucked its fill of
nectar the bee may buzz off to another flower of the
same type. If the new flower has a female stigma, the
pollen from the first
flower will stick to it.
From there the pollen
finds its way down a
special tube to the
ovaries and so
fertilises or pollinates
the female egg-cells of
the second plant.

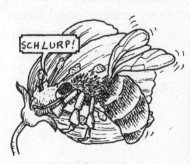

SCHLURP!

Going solo

Some plants can reproduce without flowers, entirely on their own. Here are some of the ways they do it.

Plants such as strawberries send out runners which then put down roots and start new plants in a ring round the old plant.

Plants like onions and daffodils grow bulbs. Bulbs are special groups of leaves, swollen with stored food from which new plants can shoot in the spring.

Plants such as potatoes grow underground stems called tubers. The potato tuber is good to eat but will develop into a new plant if given a chance.

SEEDS AND THINGS

Once the pollen has fertilised the egg-cell, a tiny plant called an embryo forms. The embryo plant has a tiny root and a tiny shoot and either one or two tiny swollen leaves 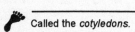 which are full of stored up food. The whole thing is then wrapped up in a hard outer coat. And there you have it - a seed. Some plants produce only a few seeds, others produce thousands. A weed called ragwort produces up to sixty-three thousand per plant.

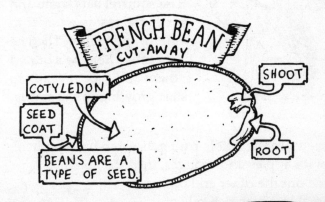

FRENCH BEAN CUT-AWAY

COTYLEDON

SHOOT

SEED COAT

ROOT

BEANS ARE A TYPE OF SEED.

At this stage the seed is still in the ovary, or fruit as it's now called - whether it's good to eat or not. The problem for the seeds is how to get out of their fruit and start a new life in the soil somewhere else. They're amazingly good at it.

STRAWBERRY

SEEDS

Called the *cotyledons*.

Seeds such as Goose grass seeds have hooks which stick to your clothes or the fur of animals, so they can be carried hundreds of miles.

Hazel nuts are designed to be forgotten by squirrels. The squirrel eats some and buries the rest in a larder to wait for the winter. Then he forgets where he's buried them and they're ready to start growing in the spring.

Sometimes the whole fruit gets eaten by an animal, as with apples and oranges, then the seeds come out the other end of the animal in a nice rich pile of dung - perfect for growing a young plant.

Some seeds, for instance thistle seeds, are so light they can float for miles.

SO THAT'S WHERE I LEFT MY NUTS!

When a seed explodes into life in the spring, in a process called *germination*, there are three things it normally needs.

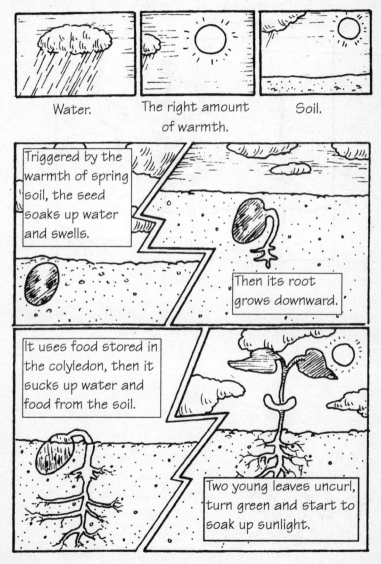

Water.

The right amount of warmth.

Soil.

Triggered by the warmth of spring soil, the seed soaks up water and swells.

Then its root grows downward.

It uses food stored in the colyledon, then it sucks up water and food from the soil.

Two young leaves uncurl, turn green and start to soak up sunlight.

Now the young plant is ready to grow seriously. Growth can be slow or incredibly fast. Some types of bamboo grow nearly a metre per day. Soon the plant is an adult and may have lots of luscious green leaves.

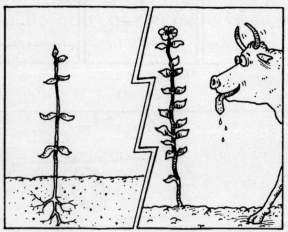

WHO EATS WHO

WHERE ARE YOU IN THE FOOD CHAIN?

Nearly all animals get their food from plants, from creatures which eat plants or from creatures which eat other creatures.

CHNOPS

CHNOPS is not the name of an Ancient Egyptian pharaoh. It's a way of remembering that all living things are made up of six main chemicals, although lots of others are also necessary for life. The main chemicals are:

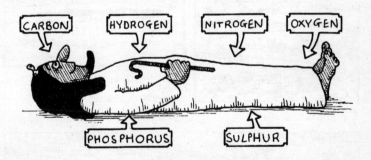

There's only a limited amount of these chemicals on planet Earth and they are always being reused as things die and get eaten. The chemicals which make up your body have been part of the bodies of countless other creatures over the years - you probably have dinosaur chemicals inside you.

THE CARBON CYCLE

There is carbon in all living things. It moves from the air into living things and back again to the air in an endless cycle. Here's one way it might happen.

Imagine. It's 100 million years ago in a damp wet forest. Two plants take carbon from carbon dioxide in the air during photosynthesis - each year Earth's plants take about 150,000 million tonnes of carbon from the air in this way.

Both plants die.

One plant gets squashed underground and slowly its remains turn into coal or oil.

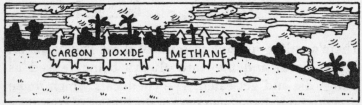

The second plant rots away. Its remains are eaten by bacteria. The bacteria breathe the carbon from its body back into the air in carbon dioxide and methane gas.

Years later during photosynthesis, another plant takes the same bit of carbon dioxide that once belonged to the second plant.

This new plant then gets eaten by an apatosaurus, which uses the carbon to build up its body weight.

A tyrannosaurus eats the apatosaurus and gets the carbon.

The tyrannosaurus dies. Its body gets eaten by bacteria as it rots away. The bacteria breathe the carbon (which the tyrannosaurus stole from the poor apatosaurus) back into the air as carbon dioxide.

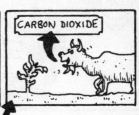

CARBON DIOXIDE

Yet another plant takes the same carbon dioxide from the air. This plant gets eaten too, but this time the animal breathes out the carbon as carbon dioxide.

The same things keep on happening for millions of years.

One day a plant in a field near you takes the same bit of carbon dioxide from the air.

A cow eats the plant.

You eat the cow. You now have carbon from the dinosaurs inside you - for the time being!

Meanwhile the plant which turned into coal has been dug up. If you have a coal fire, you may put the lump of coal containing the remains of the plant on your fire. The fire releases the carbon dioxide from the plant back into the air, ready to rejoin the carbon cycle.

THE FOOD CHAIN

Nearly all the food energy for the living things on planet Earth comes from plants, because only plants take their energy directly from sunshine.

Animals which eat plants are called *herbivores*.

Animals which eat only meat are called *carnivores*, and animals which catch and eat other animals are called *predators*.

Animals which eat both meat and plants, like us, are called *omnivores*.

THRUSH

Animals which eat the dead remains of other creatures are called *scavengers*.

VULTURE

Bacteria and fungi are called *decomposers*.

A food chain is a whole group of plants and animals, each species gobbling up the next species down the chain. Usually there are lots of small creatures at one end of the food chain and a handful of big ones at the other.

The food chain is great if you're doing the eating, but not so great if you get eaten. Animals have evolved in a great many ways to avoid being eaten. Here are a few of them.

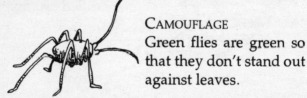

CAMOUFLAGE
Green flies are green so that they don't stand out against leaves.

PRICKLES
When hedgehogs roll up in a ball they are safe from most predators ✏.

 Clever foxes can learn how to open a curled up hedgehog.

ARMOUR

Snails and tortoises are protected by their shells.

ANYONE AT HOME?

LIE DOWN AND DON'T MOVE

Many animals will freeze in one position if they are in danger from a predator. This makes it less likely that they will be spotted.

RUN FOR YOUR LIFE!

Many herbivores are very fast runners.

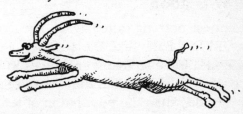

COPY A DANGEROUS ANIMAL

The hover fly looks very like a wasp, so many predators avoid it, although it doesn't really have a sting.

GOING ROTTEN

Normally big animals eat smaller animals, but when they die it tends to be the other way around. Rotting is what happens when dead tissue gets eaten by microscopic creatures and fungi.

Look at any piece of soil with a microscope and you will find that it's crawling with microscopic plants, bacteria and fungi which live off dead things which fall on the ground. There are billions of microbes in the soil - in one teaspoon of soil there can be twice as many microbes as there are people in the whole world. These tiny creatures break down the chemicals in dead things. The chemicals can then be reused by plants, starting the whole food chain off again.

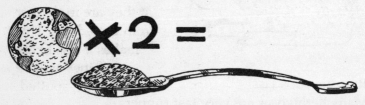

ROT IS GOOD

Suppose nothing rotted away. The living world would grind to a halt. Take the anchovy, a small fish. There are said to be so many anchovies in the ocean off the coast of California that they produce more toilet waste every day than the population of ten cities the size of Los Angeles. Imagine what would happen if none of it rotted away!

People would cause the same sort of problems as anchovies if our waste did not rot away. We use microbes to rot our sewage in sewage farms. Without them it would collect in horrible great lakes and mountains or swash around in the sea for ever. If we didn't all die of disease, most of us would probably die of disgust.

HOME SWEET HOME

A PLACE FOR EVERYONE

Since Fiona first sloshed in the warm salty water of the early ocean (if she did), life has spread to almost every nook and cranny on the surface of the Earth. There are creatures who live in the depths of the oceans where no light penetrates and there are bacteria which live on the edges of volcanoes.

Where a creature lives is called its *habitat*. Each type of creature has evolved to get the best it can out of its special habitat. Usually whole groups of animals and plants have evolved together so that a woodland habitat has woodland creatures, a desert habitat has desert creatures, and so on.

HABITAT-HOLIDAY

These animals come from several different habitats. They have got muddled up at the swimming pool during their summer holidays. Can you work out where they have come from?

WHITE FUR

EXTRA LAYER OF FAT FOR KEEPING WARM.

TAIL TO HELP CLIMB TREES

STRIPES LOOK LIKE DAPPLED SUNLIGHT.

HUMP FOR STORING WATER

Answers

White fur of polar bear gives camouflage in the snow. Tiger's stripes look like dappled sunlight in forests. Camel's hump stores water for long desert journeys. Penguin's extra layer of fat keeps it warm in the freezing cold. Tail helps monkey to climb trees in the jungle.

HAB A WARM WINTER

Habitats don't all stay the same all the year round. Many habitats are a lot colder in winter than in summer, and winter's the time of year when many animals die. Here are some things they can do to stay alive:

MIGRATE
Many insect-eating birds fly to a warmer climate to find food.

HIBERNATE
By falling into a state like a long deep sleep, animals don't use up much energy and so don't need much food. Most hibernating animals put on extra fat before they go to sleep for the winter, so that they can survive without eating.

BE AN EGG OR A CHRYSALIS
Many young insects stay in their egg or chrysalis until spring. There are not many adult insects which can survive a cold winter.

GROW MORE FUR
If you have a cat, have you noticed that it grows extra fur in the autumn and sheds it again in the spring? (Human hair grows more in the autumn, too, but it's less obvious because there's less of it.)

Homeless truth

Most of the creatures and plants in a habitat-group need each other. Kill off all the greenfly on your rosebush and the ladybirds may starve. Kill off the ladybirds and too many greenfly will breed, and they may kill the rosebush by overeating. A habitat and all the creatures and plants which live in it and off each other is called an *ecosystem*.

Perhaps the easiest way to kill off a species is to destroy its habitat: destroy your rosebush and the greenfly that lived on it will probably die. Destroy your garden and *everything* living in it may die.

Unfortunately that's what people are doing. Except that in this country it's not gardens we're digging up, it's hedgerows, woods and wild grassland. Every new road that's built, every new supermarket on a greenfield site, means less space for wild creatures.

Throughout the world people are killing off species.

You think tigers are dangerous? If they're so dangerous, how come they're nearly extinct? Look in the mirror - you're looking at the most dangerous animal on earth.

GOOD NIGHT

WHAT THE FUTURE MAY HOLD

THE MIDNIGHT HOUR

Some creatures have evolved to live by night. Many of them have big eyes to collect as much light as possible.

But the night they live in is nothing compared to the endless night which would kill all living things if the Sun stopped shining. Without the Sun to warm it, the Earth would be frozen in endless dark winter. There would be no day, no seasons, no weather and no plants to collect the extra energy needed to make food for the rest of us.

GOOD MORNING

The Earth has circled the Sun roughly four thousand million times since Fiona first sloshed about in the ocean. That's four thousand million years. It may well circle it for at least as long again. So the Sun won't stop shining for a while yet.

Since it has taken four thousand million years for you to evolve from Fiona into what you are today - what will humans look like in the distant future?

INDEX

Now Read On

If you want to know more about life and living things, see if your local library or bookshop has these books.

INSIDE STORY
By Mike Lambourne (Cassell 1993). This book tells you all you need to know about the human body - and a lot more! Find out the real low-down on how our bodies tick.

THE USBORNE ILLUSTRATED DICTIONARY OF BIOLOGY
By Corinne Stockley (Usborne Publishing Ltd.). This book is crammed full of fascinating facts and figures about life and living things. You could say, there's enough stuff on life in this book to last a lifetime!

WORM'S EYE VIEW
By Kipchak Johnson (Cassell 1990). A look at life and living things from the viewpoint of a small scruffy patch of land. Vital reading for lovers of toads, weeds - and worms, of course.

JUNGLE
By Theresa Greenaway, Eye Witness Guides Series (Dorling Kindersley). A gripping account of the plants and animals in a tropical rain forest, with spectacular photographs.

About the Author

Bob Fowke is a well-known author of children's information books. Writing under various pen names and with various friends and colleagues, he has created around fifty unusual and entertaining works on all manner of subjects.

There's always more to Fowke books than meets the eye - so don't be misled by the humorous style (just check out the index at the end of this book!). They're just the thing if you want your brain to bulge and your information banks to burble.

Bob Fowke is the youngest son of a Sussex vicar, and spent his childhood in the large, draughty vicarage of the village of Fletching (where the famous historian Edward Gibbon is buried). After years of travel and adventure, he now lives quietly in Shropshire.

OTHER BOOKS IN THIS SERIES

QUEEN VICTORIA, HER FRIENDS AND RELATIONS by Fred Finney. This book digs the dirt on the dumpy little lady in black.

HENRY VIII, HIS FRIENDS AND RELATIONS by Fred Finney. All you never knew about the man who preferred the executioner's axe to the divorce courts!

PIRATES OF THE PAST by Jim Hatfield. What life was really like beneath the Jolly Roger!

VILLAINS THROUGH THE AGES by Jim Hatfield. There are bad guys, and there are very bad guys. This book is about the very, very bad ones.

SHAKESPEARE by Anita Ganeri. What the brilliant bard and his mad mates were really like.

ANCIENT EGYPTIANS by David Jay. They used monkeys to arrest burglars!

ELIZABETH I, HER FRIENDS AND RELATIONS by Bob Fowke. What life was really like when men wore their knickers outside their tights.

VIKINGS by Bob Fowke. Fancy a bowl of blood soup before bedtime?

WORLD WAR II by Bob Fowke. Who won the War, and why men didn't have jacket pockets.

SCIENCE by Bob Fowke. Enough to drive a mad scientist madder.